THE FIRE PASSAGE

Also by Lisa Wells

Believers

The Fix

THE FIRE PASSAGE

Lisa Wells

Four Way Books
Tribeca

For the Speaker of the dream

Library of Congress Cataloging-in-Publication Data

Names: Wells, Lisa, 1982–author.
Title: Fire passage / Lisa Wells.
Description: New York : Four Way Books, 2025.
Identifiers: LCCN 2024035153 (print) | LCCN 2024035154 (ebook) | ISBN 9781961897366 (trade paperback) | ISBN 9781961897373 (ebook)
Subjects: LCGFT: Poetry.
Classification: LCC PS3623.E4755 F57 2025 (print) | LCC PS3623.E4755 (ebook) | DDC 811/.6–dc23/eng/20240809
LC record available at https://lccn.loc.gov/2024035153
LC ebook record available at https://lccn.loc.gov/2024035154

This book is manufactured in the United States of America and printed on acid-free paper.

Funding for this book was provided in part by a generous donation in memory of John J. Wilson.

Four Way Books is a not-for-profit literary press. We are grateful for the assistance we receive from individual donors, public arts agencies, and private foundations including the NEA, and the New York State Council on the Arts, a state agency.

We are a proud member of the Community of Literary Magazines and Presses.

Contents

"The fascinated individual hears *the call of the funeral pyre*. For him destruction is more than a change, it is a renewal."

—Gaston Bachelard, *The Psychoanalysis of Fire*

"The descent to hell is easy; day and night the gates are open. But to retrace your steps and reach the air above—there's the rub, the task."

—Virgil, *The Aeneid*

THE FLOODS

0.

They prefer that I speak plainly. No tricks. I can sympathize.

I was sick, plainly.
I had my symptoms.

Physicians of every age and bedside manner tested my blood, stool, saliva, and with a look that becomes familiar to medical-mysteries and the malingering alike, they communicated their skeptical pity.

As if the wound were in my mind.
And it was. But it was elsewhere, too.

Bathed in the light of their disbelief
I could touch the whole history.

So the wound is a window?

Yes
and no.

I.

Clicked home an unknown way through the city.

Past the bread factory's glassy nave
where conveyors parade whole white loaves
and acrid sweetness humps the air.

Is this the waking world? Alive in the shadows
of great paneláks, clean as sun-bleached femurs.

And the song of haggling in the stalls.
Odor of syrup and unwashed sex
unlocked from hunks of perspiring mālum.

Which of our hands fingered this fruit first?

2.

I recall, the shaggy seer said
    Truth is the god that wants it.

I held that song in my ears to the exclusion of all others.

Mists, rolling over the headland
bring trembling to the palm fronds

raise dysenterious floods
to the lips of bridges, ornately carved.

Tell me, who's going to love us now
that we hasten the epoch?

3.

Smocked in a paper bib, I packed
a rattle in my lung to the sanitarium.

The delicate nurse spooned my soil into a vial.
It will culture in a day.

Just think, something of me grows in silence
as we speak.
          It's a godly feeling

to flip the light switch
    watch the frightened roaches scatter.

Shake the roaches from my loafers and slip
into the corridor for refreshment.

Change jangling spooks the other patients from their rooms.

I love the way the can slams the vendor's internal workings.

And the artifice of the rectory
impressed upon my eye a phrase:

          The fear of the Lord is the beginning of knowledge.

4.

Replace the days with such phrases
for one who tramps in the midst of illness.

Turned out by the body.
Malignancy's forced pilgrimage.

      First, they will lead us down a hall
and fit us in their nightmare chair—

tied off to the metronomic drip of radiant chemical.

Friend, we die, but do not die alone.

It comes for all?

It comes for all.

5.

And we fear the troubled hours
of Earth. To be ridden by that

famous tide of rapturous woe.
But this is just the gap between

the platform and the door. The dead are
at this very moment speeding back.

6.

Goddamn it's hot in the afterlife.
Equanimous light throws the flesh a steady glow
and there's rarely ever wind.

I say, there's rarely any sound at all.

Caterpillars inch along the tile
flashing with light from the refineries.

Pick up my ears at the lip and listen
to power whine through the grid.

Our houses built on stilts
to accommodate the floods.

    Strange vertigo at sea level. Panic skips
its mordents through my blood.

7.

I had complaints.
I wanted more than I was given.

In line at Loaves and Fishes for the paper-sack allowance.
    Top Ramen, Carnation powdered milk
and sweet Wonder bread (green in a day).

Nevertheless, I devour my handout
then ride my lover on the kitchen linoleum.
Eat, fuck, sleep, repeat.

I am one in a circle of hideous women
rumored to mate on the first date.

Here too,
Our Lady of Frosted Roots.
Our Lady of Junk-Induced Sepsis.

We've got an easy way with proverb.

    *In the land of gangrenous amputation
the abscessed man is king.*

8.

So the seer said: *The Lord don't like nothin' too tall.*

He cuts you down to size
He cuts you down to size

All the world's a game of limbo.
I never know how low I'll go.
I don't believe I'll reach the bottom.

9.

From *vaca* came *vaccination.*
From the smooth hands of the milkmaids came
this coterie of itinerant inoculators.

From the daguerreotype:
sores, in precise succession, throbbing along
a child's spine like the buttoned closure of a dress.

Take this image from my eye.

It is taken.

10.

Cadavers mug for the observer
    tucked inside the camera's accordion,
flies mobbing their menses.

Bad move to shut your eyes
for the gaze of the microscopist is
ever inward.

Arranged an audience with the deranged anatomist
to contemplate one transverse section of the whole:

the collection of enzymes and substrates that make a man
tick-tock.

The room was a butcher's shop.

    A man pinioned by mooring stakes,
        suppurated flesh pulled away
    like yellowing rolls of gauze

as if, flayed
the man were *more* himself.

II.

I always assumed I'd be smothered in sleep with a hospital pillow.
An up-tempo monitor giving way to sustain.

That scene in the thriller always plays.

Who wants to go out
pacing the cage of a high-security campus?

Locked down in a stairwell
with my demagnetized swipe-card

amidst the intervening
            sirens and silences

cellular rupture and the spectacle of spring
all together now.

Stood rapt in the aftershock
worrying a comb of bone.

12.

Is it Eden I long for?
A bayou at dusk, glitzy with fireflies
    where rising tides arouse the wharves.

I am engirdled in the plastic rings
of every sixer I ever shotgunned.

Reliving the all-day drunks,
fucked thrice before sundown.

My nostalgia stumps me.

13.

In life, I was rigid.
I had a treatment plan.

I had a prism. It bent the light.
I mistook it for vision.

At last, peeled back the cataract
        to admit to my iris this image
of slender black branches stroked by lichen.

Lord, what I have loved was frail
but freighted with deep time.

My first language was memory.
The skin of my face my manuscript.

14.

And I was the mangy bitch proceeding
from a feldspar quarry. My leash removed.

I came upon the colophon of the underworld:

      You will meet, on the road, a man
      of mechanical passions
      whose right eye is a lens
      whose left eye is its image

      whose companion is
      a stray coyote, guardian of the wash

      bringing news of the slaughtering block
            as even the slaughterers abominate
      the maggots living on their heirs.

After several months' disintegration
    the raiment proves obedience to the corpse.

We will be tested by many mouths.

15.

Things go surpassingly well
behind the locked gate of the leprosarium.

Sunflowers burst high above the walls
        and the wives of Leschi
 host a tennis clinic every other Monday.

It is quite agreeable
here in the tangle
under a peach umbrella.

Waiter, I have tasted your angelica
        now bring me your finest purgative, up.

Bring the leftovers of the pot, a spray of your Binaca
        and play for me again that song

        After you get what you want,
You don't want what you wanted at all—

        I sip my tonic on the veranda and bask
        in the leper clapper's tympanic ramble . . .

I am as Gilgamesh among cedars!
Armed only with my chisel set
        for the trepanation.

See it now?
>	*What no dead dog will eat*
>	she eats.

I have diagnosed this community's disease:
stagnation in extremities.

16.

in extremis, I was
a figure on a path.
A stranger recruited from an eave

at the World's Largest Truck Stop.
I held a styrofoam cup of instant coffee
and my dog-eared volume of Common Prayer.

Called out by a circle of children
huddled over a baby rattler

       with percussive uprush a sudden
flight of mice to the mesquite.

Their keeper was a blowsy girl in Princess Leia buns.
She swooned on the arm of her bigamist,
both amply dosed.

       The plunge of her dress revealed
     breasts, sorely wealed

and the site consumed me—as the chili plucks
    the bud—did this girl arouse
       such a stutter in my function.

17.

Stripped down to the greaves I strode
into the weedy field behind the Men's.

And there emerged the one called "Mouth"
obstreperous little shit
as squat and stacked as a Swiss Army knife.

I said, "What do you stand for, Mouth?"

Next thing I know we're wounding the poppy
for an ooze of its milky sap.

Made banquet of opioid, watercress, wormwood.

Could have been a week that passed
or several minutes.

18.

The Mouth unleashed his coated tongue,
his wad of sweet gum, scant hair
from a black-tailed deer.

Such pharmacopic sorcery was never seen.
I seized in an orgiastic rear

    at the knee of the next world
where several visions commenced.

. . . a woman stalled at the threshold with a ripe plum.

. . . a scrap of scarlet on the nuptial bed.

Lucid dream this
seems so lifelike

my mild pastoral hope
grown timorous.

Wake me when my quaking's done.

THE FIRE PASSAGE

o.

I locked the door on the seventh floor of the otherwise empty
dormitory and appraised, through its window, the grid below.

Activity populated the aperture, but even that resisted conclusion.

I don't mean this figuratively.
I mean there is a window in a locked room on the tower's
seventh floor and it is high enough to wreak actual havoc.

I mean it would be possible to impose a narrative conclusion on
my confusion of symptoms.

Plainly. I both lived in terror of my disease and daydreamed of dying.
An unoriginal paradox.

I lived in terror and I loved the world.
A fire meanwhile rising.

19.

First, I had a jackal in my genus.
Then I moved among branches, nimbly.

Rose to my feet in the Pleistocene
to fulfill the homo-schematic

of hair, backbone, milk production,
musculature and motion of limbs.

Peaked in these tobacco-stained folds of chintz
when Moses parted the drapery

and a pearl-handled switchblade
tapped the glass

Come out, come out, and admit the blade!

Now's the day I pay the piper.

Now's the plague of sulfured egg.

20.

In order to test the tensile strength
of the resource chain

we sewed a housebroken seed
and sprouted the singularity.

Blight latched the new buds.
Peril unwound in strangling vines.

My mother called it *widowmaker,*
that blackened snag that forked my sight

and hatched the spore that mapped this
archipelago of blood onto my handkerchief.

I long to live again
in a murmur of larvae, of bioluminescence

in dentrical arms of radiolaria.
An ordinary being should be consecrated.

21.

Through pressure and momentum—
like clay turned on a wheel—my Lord forms me.

Was it His hands that shaped the charismatic megafauna
and rendered cryptic the phylliidae?

I tied my wrist to the branch
to pacify His ghost

but the boughs interlaced
and the canopy closed.

Subsisting, now, on the dark understory.

> It might be interesting to see what I look like.
> But I can never get into that shaft of light
>   that creeps in this cave, because the people
>   block my way—

Bored a wound, in time, into the escarpment
for I wanted to sleep off the dream.

Please permit no more
fear into my temple.

I should have been a better friend to myself.

22.

Freed from the herd but who am I?
Why so restless?

Steady drums of primer herald
a textureless world.

I wanted to punish the principals
who dropped their pigs on our oak groves
ate up the acorn and starved us out

but the beasts would not lie down.
Made a pig eater of me.

Two fingers tilt back the chin
the other hand draws the blade.

Another's hand holds the catching bowl
but all our lips sip of this.

23.

Emerging from terra incognita
one morning before the fall

came the aroma of pulp mills
and the means to feed.

When I'm eating bread
I sense I'm close to the capital.

Babylon falls suddenly and is broken.

Rise and collapse, ad infinitum—
we know the drill.

I was promised to these phlegmatic elites.
All along the trace

shock troops trail a whiff of the morgue,
and the Battle Hymn of the prick ischemic.

I was their working girl, yes,
but didn't prod myself into their bed

nor offer my eyes to their veil.

Nor did I refuse these advances.

24.

Who will quell the throng that scourged
each encountered kingdom?

Early on, I heard *rota tu volubilis*
and resolved
            to break attachment to the body

of viscous oil fueling me through Laughlin,
            Nevada: asshole of the planet
                        home of the newlywed and nearly dead

into the pure blazing threat of the county

        whereupon I picked a song
out of the static

        yeah *I Got Friends in Low Places*

25.

My rods and cones were seemingly designed
for that jaundiced light at last call.

Closing out,
my face grows actual.

Wasn't the whole point of getting wasted
dilation?

Sex on the beach, sweet pink umbrella
piercing the flesh of the maraschino.

I thought to tongue-tie the stem,
to become a warm and dim circumference.

My suitor limped into the bar, one hand sheltering a candle.

He extinguished the wick suggestively
then held my tongue
and I prayed to my Lord

> *Lord, he's a burr in my brain.*
> *Yoke me to this other*

26.

But another beauty queen sidled close.

Miss Weyerhaeuser '99. Her spray-hard bangs
curled and teased like fine breaking waves.

They must have dragged the floor of hell to surface that piece.

"Darlin'," she said. "Your dimples are unfair.
 Show me that wiggle-ass dance you do."

Bedraggled babygirl
        Of those so close beside me, which are you?

27.

It is the pliant way, to bow
to the ones who unwittingly left
the child in bed with the pedophile.

In the unfortunate dive bar of daughters
descendent of daughters
you must dance with the one that brung you.

It was another life, on the highway shoulder
bent in scrap grass collecting
orphaned cans and bottles.

I ate with a mouth, excreted with an anus,
constraints given me before the breaking.

And the breaking is a means
of sparing a woman her own construction.

28.

At the end of my shaking
I diapered my groin and sang

over arid clay. My song goes
soaring above the shrill

notes of the tweak pipe
and its ravaged player.

Who twists out a paste
of redneck cocaine with his pestle.

Whose jittering song will lead
the children into the sea.

Whose throne is draped in a train of entrail
made vague by heat and duration.

Yikes.

I'd like to come back to life
but don't yet know the way.

29.

I call my dead by name.
In my thought
they clot

> *The people, in here, are large, enormous.*
> *They echo themselves when they talk.*
> *And their shadows, on the cave walls,*
>   *follow them, as they move*

At myself again.
The Derider mocks my form in clay.

You know that slag.
She'd dwell as much on her own filth
as on the beauty around her

And yet, I remain
dazzled by motes in a shaft of ordinary light

and by contrails unwinding in the trade wind
though they think me dim.

30.

This incessant posturing will cease. The thin intellect
        bleeds through the fissures of the mind
and bright lucidity dawns.

The old way is done.

Under fluorescence we are stripped,
washed, and wrapped in the Eslene.

Platters of saltines and pudding are placed
upon the gingham, and how this show fatigues.

This is the prisoner's cinema.
No light enters the eye and yet
it marbles at the threshold

condenses in the depression where I
patiently abide my illness

angling for the one who would touch
the self inside myself.

And where's my suitor now?
I called and called

Room 549 of the Belmont Hotel.

The emergency dispatch confirmed

I'm here.

Hello?

I'm here.

31.

Born again on a Monday
under a broken zodiac.

My father the woodman, a surgeon among snags,
could read the living trail of blades
rebounding in the field

that mopped-matte passage
through the dew.

He woke a brush pile with fire
throwing shadows on the child.

I was thrown over.

Father, it was a pleasure to meet you
on this luminous route between two lives

in this impromptu pool reaped from rain
where mosquitos multiply.

Though survival, I'm told, is impersonal
and without teleological purpose.

Malaria is just trying to maximize its own fitness.
As are the corporate-persons who

for palm oil set the peatlands ablaze
and drained the water table.

Dense haze from the sea
choked the light from day

suffused our mountain
in a numinous red corona.

And as for the getting over
there will be no ascension

no circumambulation
there is only going through.

We must go through it.

SPELLS FOR ASCENDING

o.

I loved the world. Was of it. Offered my wounded song
to the midnight dog

but what came through me was not plain or even decent.

You know. You've come this far.

Like the eager anatomist, the poet, too
is "parasitic upon the dead."

And yet the dead don't seem to mind.
Not when your hand's outstretched.

For the spell, I came to see, is also an ark.

32.

I was an infant.
I came of age.

And sometime gleaned my earthly purpose
was to ease the loneliness of men.

But to ease the loneliness of men, I had
to hide my priapic drive within.

Now, as I strive to sleep I hear
    the burning of the sedge
        splintering of fallen alders

        and unfixed from garden beds
green-bursting sulfur clouds,
        comingling of mercury, salt, and the sheer
mass of decaying matter.

What I knew before
I'm trying to remember.

Dense growths of epiphytes, marbled murrelets,
        lynx and wolverine, herbaceous anodynes.

Already dead, yet
have scarcely felt more alive.

33.

All cruelty done away.
Nothing's lonely now, nothing anymore in pain

Are these specters circled in my train?

Fresh-faced, the exalted corpse
stands up and lives.

I've come to wash that pilgrim's feet.

34.

Pilgrim, have you lately asked
what am I for?

To what purpose should I apply this borrowed corpus?

I desired to write a history of the wound
but it is.

We used to gather at the rim to weep into the crater.
Not filling it was the point.

mecum omnes plangite

for the old gods demoted to idols
in the drive toward unification.

Turned out I'd given my life to something too small.
Bilked by the bad pastor who asked
Which master do you serve?

Answer.
I served a derivative daddy-type.

Control was the chief delusion.
Numbed-out in managing
total compliance to the incursive agenda.

Went along to get along
and the hand that wounded me was my own.

35.

Surrender to the thought that knows
it is thinking.

Zero in on the locus, take the imago in

          ingest it, ingest its
questions:

What plot in this?
What balm on the aggrieved?
What fear underneath?
When were we blessed?

36.

In the idle evening, the Morning Star
moved in me.

A bright skiff rocking in the blear.

That Which spoke the dream into my ear
spoke out of my body
spoke *me* out.

Now I hold its chop in my mouth,
and in my folds
the sacred Nehalem River flows.

There is a path there, flanked
by hemlocks in mossy capes

and from those bodies in congress I learned
              the way of the twinning branch
how each twig helps each
twig to light.

Ruckus of wind in the aspens
was the music piped into me.

At night, a nougat moon
rose low over the caldera
        ridged by mountains soft as thighs.

A girl could lie in that light,
        singing with her female companions

                and I did want to.
As the spider dances in her web would I.

37.

On the seventh day I saw the concrete breached,
the river returned to its original vein, and pulsing there
slick and muscular multitudes
          of coho winding north to spawn.

It was so.

I understood intuitively, if the salmon are to return
I must maim the developer's trademark.

Now here comes the Prince of Fractured Libido
          and his purse dog, Chip.

Here's our man, the Viceroy of Bitumen
   also known as
      "He who bloviates well into the lunch hour."

Not quite a circle of hell.
More like a coffee ring

their restless feet treadling beneath a conference table
while the talking heads outline

their suicidal mission:
          Strip the mountain, burn the slash.

I vow to banish these knuckleheads
just as soon as I get born again.

            In a scabby motel off I-80
amidst air-conditioned doldrums
the dream began

dream of the magnetic pole
     conductive of sun's
          clockwise action and counter-
          clockwise action of moon-

gears of equal and opposite force manifest
          violet thunderheads, lightning-crazed
traveling out from the center in concentric rings
          to make a world.

This is the logic of resistance.

38.

We will greet, on the road to Tar Sands, a man
of myriad chattering heads—addicted
to the freebased recremental whee of implosion.

Who has, for an opponent,
the meeting of middle-class reformists.

Are you waiting for the thrill jockey to get his fill
and climb down off us?

> *He will never get his fill.*
> *He will never climb down off us.*

Just ask the kids at Fort Mac
        where threshers undo
    the true name of Lake Athabasca.

Forgone, that we were all accomplice
        but it's not too late to turn
        if you want to

cool your heels here on Earth.

39.

Go, for they call you, pilgrim
up from the sweat-drenched ticking
under ceiling fans cutting slow through your sleep.

Go, to your street of disrepair
where the flock of mourners waits
keening on the lawn.

The dogs all gone to rest,
their skeletons refuse
       the slackening of hide, time

and through the moon-blanched green I plan
to shoot another tendril.

For I was a reaper in a field of rushes
my scythe adored the hidden forms
leaning backward in the dream

      but the grasses moved away from me

40.

and live murmurs there
of flesh transgressed by worms.

This human way is abrupt as a brick shithouse
but down in that dismal pit the slag
fosters heaps of flowers.

What unearned imprimatur
gave us skin to touch another?

I have known you in this life.

Have purred in your spell of soft, abstracted air.
Turned once to watch you cross a stile
into a public way

     Thou hast not lived, why shouldst thou perish, so?

41.

So dawned the final confrontation.
A bruise in unus mundus.

Vistas of stump and sumac.
And fires raging east of the mountain send
     refugee smoke
          to settle on the coastal strand.

Go take your shelter there.

Deep shade unfolds
from hush of chufa
and bracken's wooly fiddleheads

under seven cedars risen
ghosts collecting in their crowns.
We will build the next life from the parting

of self and object; from lomatium's crinoline slips
and fields of wild hyacinth

under a lattice, skinned and sewn over with stars, oh say
     and say again the names
of the departed.

42.

I peered into the urn
and saw the mutant lymph go clear.
The tumor—mere pea—forked by a single tine.

Certain figures, unknown to me in life, appeared
        and spoke aloud a spell for ascending

            through dream and speech made same
                the lifeless are alive again

Where iron dropped, compressed, condensed,
        core began, heat decayed, structure razed,
raised the skin we move upon, and rivers vein the skin.

    Where snails made the stone brocade, stone brocaded
riverbank and banked a stony gibbous moon
        to pulse this frock of light estranged.

Where mind was child's and fear was night
            night seeped the peeping stars
light estranged from sun decayed
            and midwives coaxed polarities

breast bled the first warm measure
    of sucrose overtaking vein
wary, sweet, expiring skin from
    where we came

I think it was—

I think it

43.

Slow seas drove one continent against another,
then the crags shelved upward.

Where taiga heaved toward tundra
a panicked swimmer turns

and overturns in its wake.

The sea lion, alone, in her cave
is barking

as the ice sheets retreat from the latitudes.
The final cycle begun.

I melt.
I freeze again.
I am that shell the chill caresses;

a glittering crust collapsed
by the slightest tap of sun.

What leaks into the breech
unmakes me, makes me new.

We think the transformation beautiful
            but it's loud inside the chrysalis.

What to do with this baroque assemblage
of glass, shale, and oyster
but speak the names?

See the dry bones leap together.

the wild seed has entered the waters
the wild lichen has masked the asphalt
the green fur has smothered the sheetrock
the green creeper has strangled the steel

        Wild seeds wild wind dispersed
      released from the holds
of warring birds—

                                    it is so.

44.

Who made the mouth speak a spell
to resurrect me?

Who knows Who
ordained that light.

Last night's touch
still singing in my skin

I wake
and need again

and needing, fear.
No one mentions the fear

of nearly touching
of reaching out for

when the reach is
interrupted.

No one mentions the injury,
their eyes find somewhere else to land.

But I was dismantled by hand.
He touched the center

sealed the binding spell
He-to-me, He bare-chested

in drawers of black cotton, sipping a sour beer.

Come here, He said, *let's have a look at you.*

45.

That Which so loved the scorpion
speaks now in the browsing of the saplings,

in cicadas' swollen unison,
tremors in the skin of the milk.

Is the beam of the Maglite sweeping
the woods beyond the off-ramp

Its broken strobe alighting
on the Beloved's recovered brow

and how it staggers, it
whispers across the lips

of bottles, swims in the vasculature
of millipedes, shoots raw into the coppice

crowned by orchids, bromeliads
upon a fallen limb's decay

upon twin monarchs' helical lifting
to wake again the sprouting bed.

In soft soil blankets It churns
It hums among detritivores

with paste of sawdust and sweet saliva
papers over the gaps in the mound.

Whose bacterial dance is vast
transubstantiation.

Who entered the steps of the human migration
trailing fruit trees and macaques.

That Which picks
through smoldering rubbish

on the banks of the new
new world. Holy scavenger

pray the deep-green palms
adapted to darkness.

Praise now pollinators,
the blind roots deeply probing

red-sexed hibiscus lanterns
and symbiotic wasps, lower than mimosa.

      Come you now, Mimosa
do not shrink from That Which

razed the scab, will
fertilize the disturbance.

Already its great wave breaks
against the mangroves.

Let us go
and greet it.

ACKNOWLEDGMENTS

Sections of this work were first published by *The Iowa Review,* the Poetry Foundation, *OmniVerse,* and *Two Peach.* Grateful acknowledgement to their editors.

Several lines are quoted from the "O Fortuna" section of the *Carmina Burana* by Carl Orf, and R. D. Laing's *The Divided Self* (principally, the testimony of "Joan"). Thank you to the R. D. Laing Estate. Section 15 quotes the *Epic of Gilgamesh* (John Gardner Ed., John Maier Tr., Vintage Books) and "After You Get What You Want, You Don't Want It," by Irving Berlin. Section 32 quotes "The Waking" by Theodore Roethke (from *The Collected Poems,* Anchor Books). Section 33 quotes "Almost Was Good Enough," by Jason Molina, published by Autumn Bird Songs (ASCAP) / Secretly Canadian Publishing (ASCAP). Used by permission. 39 and 40 are after Matthew Arnold's "The Scholar-Gypsy." Other informing influences include correspondence with Zach Savich, lectures by Mira Seo and William Piel, *The Healing Hand: Man and Wound in the Ancient World* by Guido Manjo, *Through the Dark Wood* by James Hollis, and *The Sick Rose* by Richard Barnett (also quoted directly on Page 43, thanks to Thames & Hudson). The opening epigraph is taken from *The Psychoanalysis of Fire* by Gaston Bachelard. Copyright © 1964 by Alan C. M. Ross. Originally published in French under the title *La Psychanalyse du Feu* Copyright © 1938 by Librairie Gallimard. Reprinted with permission from Beacon Press, Boston Massachusetts.

Thanks to Daniel Poppick and Jessica Laser for helpful feedback, and to the initial readers who pushed this book forward.

Immense gratitude to Diane Seuss for choosing it, to Four Way Books and Ryan Murphy, for making it real, and to Rowan Sharp for making it better.

I was saved by the wounded music of orphans, outcasts, and addicts. Thanks to my friends. I bow to my sisters Prudence Johnston, Hana Andronikova, and Jenny Brouwer, whose beauty and magnetism pulled me into the passage. Thanks most of all to Joshua Marie Wilkinson and to Jude, whose love pulls me through.

About the Author

Lisa Wells is a poet, nonfiction writer, and editor. Her debut collection, *The Fix*, won the Iowa Poetry Prize. Her most recent book, *Believers* (FSG) was a finalist for the PEN/E.O. Wilson Literary Science Writing Award. Her work has been published in *Harper's Magazine, Granta, The New York Times*, and *Orion*, and has been anthologized in *The Best American Science and Nature Writing* and *The Best American Food and Travel Writing*. She lives in Portland, Oregon with Joshua Marie Wilkinson and their son. Together they serve as editors for the Kuhl House Poets Series at the University of Iowa Press.

WE ARE ALSO GRATEFUL TO THOSE INDIVIDUALS WHO PARTICIPATED IN
OUR BUILD A BOOK PROGRAM. THEY ARE:

Anonymous (14), Robert Abrams, Debra Allbery, Nancy Allen,
Michael Ansara, Kathy Aponick, Jean Ball, Sally Ball, Jill Bialosky,
Sophie Cabot Black, Laurel Blossom, Tommye Blount, Karen and
David Blumenthal, Jonathan Blunk, Lee Briccetti, Jane Martha Brox,
Mary Lou Buschi, Anthony Cappo, Carla and Steven Carlson,
Robin Rosen Chang, Liza Charlesworth, Peter Coyote,
Elinor Cramer, Kwame Dawes, Michael Anna de Armas,
Brian Komei Dempster, Renko and Stuart Dempster,
Matthew DeNichilo, Rosalynde Vas Dias, Patrick Donnelly,
Charles R. Douthat, Lynn Emanuel, Blas Falconer, Laura Fjeld,
Carolyn Forché, Helen Fremont and Donna Thagard,
Debra Gitterman, Dorothy Tapper Goldman, Alison Granucci,
Elizabeth T. Gray Jr., Naomi Guttman and Jonathan Mead,
Jeffrey Harrison, KT Herr, Carlie Hoffman, Melissa Hotchkiss,
Thomas and Autumn Howard, Catherine Hoyser, Elizabeth Jackson,
Linda Susan Jackson, Jessica Jacobs, Deborah Jonas-Walsh,
Jennifer Just, Voki Kalfayan, Maeve Kinkead, Victoria Korth,
David Lee and Jamila Trindle, Rodney Terich Leonard,
Howard Levy, Owen Lewis and Susan Ennis, Eve Linn,
Matthew Lippman, Ralph and Mary Ann Lowen, Maja Lukic,
Neal Lulofs, Anthony Lyons, Ricardo Alberto Maldonado,
Trish Marshall, Donna Masini, Deborah McAlister, Carol Moldaw,
Michael and Nancy Murphy, Kimberly Nunes, Matthew Olzmann and
Vievee Francis, Veronica Patterson, Patrick Phillips, Robert Pinsky,
Megan Pinto, Kevin Prufer, Anna Duke Reach, Paula Rhodes,
Yoana Setzer, James Shalek, Soraya Shalforoosh, Peggy Shinner,
Joan Silber, Jane Simon, Debra Spark, Donna Spruijt-Metz,
Arlene Stang, Page Hill Starzinger, Catherine Stearns,
Yerra Sugarman, Arthur Sze, Laurence Tancredi, Marjorie and
Lew Tesser, Peter Turchi, Connie Voisine, Susan Walton,
Martha Webster and Robert Fuentes, Calvin Wei, Allison Benis White,
Lauren Yaffe, and Rolf Yngve.